THE POWER OF
Praying™ Together
PRAYER CARDS

STORMIE OMARTIAN

HARVEST HOUSE™ PUBLISHERS

EUGENE, OREGON

THE POWER OF PRAYING™ TOGETHER PRAYER CARDS
Copyright © 2003 by Stormie Omartian
Published by Harvest House Publishers
Eugene, Oregon 97402
www.harvesthousepublishers.com

ISBN 0-7369-1071-9

Printed in Hong Kong

03 04 05 06 07 08 09 / NG-CF / 10 9 8 7 6 5 4 3 2 1

INTRODUCTION

$\mathcal{I}$t may seem strange to pray about learning how to pray, but the precedent for that was set with Jesus' disciples. They specifically asked Jesus to teach them how to pray. And so should we. These prayer cards will not only assist you in doing that, but they will also help you to *acknowledge your dependence* on God, *communicate your needs* to Him, and *submit your life* to the Lord in such a way that you can be a vessel through whom He can work in power. We can't move into all the freedom, fulfillment, purpose, and blessing God has for us if we don't make certain that we have put Him in the driver's seat of our lives. These prayers will help you to do that as they encourage you to depend on God's power to touch the situations you care about, instead of depending on your own strength and resources.

The prayers on these cards can be prayed during your intimate devotional time with the Lord, and in the process I hope they will serve as a reminder of more personal ways you can pray about specific needs in your own life. Or they can be prayed with a prayer partner or group as a starting point for more in-depth group prayer. Whichever way you use them, whether alone or with others, they will help you move with specific focus into more powerful prayer times.

I pray that each of your prayers will be followed by God's blessing of answered prayer in dimensions you have never seen before.

—*Stormie Omartian*

Lord, I realize I am powerless to do anything of significance or accomplish anything lasting without You. I know it is not by my strength or wisdom that powerful things happen in my life, but it is by Your Spirit. My prayers are not answered because of *what* I know, but because of *whom* I know. I'm grateful that I know You.

❧ ❧ ❧

"Not by might nor by power, but by My Spirit,"
says the LORD *of hosts.*

ZECHARIAH 4:6

FILL ME WITH YOUR HOLY SPIRIT

*L*ord, thank You for saving me and setting me free from all that would keep me from moving into everything You have for me. Thank You for filling me with Your Holy Spirit and loving me into wholeness.

～ ～ ～

The love of God has been poured out in our hearts by the Holy Spirit who was given to us.

ROMANS 5:5

YOU'RE MY SOURCE OF POWER

*H*oly Spirit, I acknowledge You this day as my source of power. I invite You to fill me afresh and flow freely through me. I know that without You I can do nothing.

∽ ∽ ∽

His divine power has given to us all things
that pertain to life and godliness, through
the knowledge of Him who called us by glory
and virtue, by which have been given to us
exceedingly great and precious promises.

2 PETER 1:3-4

TEACH ME IN ALL THINGS

*H*oly Spirit, I rely on You to do beyond all that I can think or imagine. Teach me in all things. Help me to understand the exceeding greatness of Your power toward us who believe (Ephesians 1:19).

∽ ∽ ∽

When He, the Spirit of truth, has come,
He will guide you into all truth.

JOHN 16:13

I WANT TO MOVE IN YOUR POWER

Lord, I want to be a person who moves in Your power
and whose prayers have the power to effect significant
change in the world around me. Help me to always
remember to live by the power of Your Spirit and not try
to do things in my own strength. Show me how to use
the keys You have given me to unlock and unleash Your
power in prayer.

～ ～ ～

I will give you the keys of the kingdom of heaven.

MATTHEW 16:19

*L*ord, You are awesome above all else on the earth. It is You, O Lord, who gives strength and power to Your people (Psalm 68:35). Thank You that Your power is mighty in us. Thank You that just as You raised Jesus from the dead, You will also raise me up by Your power (1 Corinthians 6:14).

～ ～ ～

God has power to help and to overthrow.

2 CHRONICLES 25:8

YOUR GRACE IS SUFFICIENT

*L*ord, thank You that Your grace is sufficient for me. That Your strength is made perfect in my weakness. I would rather boast in my infirmities, so that the power of Christ rests upon me (2 Corinthians 12:9). God, You are my strength and power. You make my way perfect. You make my feet like the feet of deer, and You set me on high places (2 Samuel 22:33-34).

~ ~ ~

And of His fullness we have all received,
and grace for grace.

JOHN 1:16

*L*ord, I thank You that You are my Savior, Healer, Redeemer, Deliverer, Provider, Counselor, and coming King. I specifically thank You that You are (name what you are most thankful for about the Lord that reflects His character).

 ↩ ↩ ↩

Give unto the LORD the glory due to His name.

PSALM 29:2

I PRESENT MY DAY TO YOU

Lord, I present my day to You and ask You to bless it in every way. I surrender all the details of it into Your hands. In everything I face today, I ask You to be with me. Give me peace in the midst of the unexpected.

～ ～ ～

Seek the kingdom of God,
and all these things shall be added to you.

LUKE 12:31

DIRECT MY PATHS

*L*ord, I trust You with all my heart, and I will not lean on my own understanding. I acknowledge You in all my ways and ask You to direct my paths (Proverbs 3:5-6). Order my day and be in charge of it. Help me to do all I need to do.

~ ~ ~

The steps of a good man are ordered by the LORD,
and He delights in his way.

PSALM 37:23

I GIVE MYSELF TO YOU AS A LIVING SACRIFICE

*L*ord, I present my body to You as a living sacrifice, holy and acceptable (Romans 12:1). Teach me how to treat it with care and be a good steward of it. Help me not to mistreat it in any way or use it improperly.

∽ ∽ ∽

You were bought at a price;
therefore glorify God in your body
and in your spirit, which are God's.

1 CORINTHIANS 6:20

YOU ARE MY HEALER

*L*ord, enable me to make good decisions with regard to maintaining healthful habits. Show me anything I need to do or stop doing that would bless my health. Specifically I pray for (name any area where you need the Lord to help you or heal you). Thank You that You are my healer.

∽ ∽ ∽

He sent His word and healed them.

PSALM 107:20

TEACH ME FROM YOUR WORD

Lord, teach me from Your Word so that I will know Your ways and walk in them. Help me to live in obedience to Your commands. Thank You that my sin does not have to separate me from You because by repenting of it and confessing it to You, I can be set free.

∽ ∽ ∽

If we confess our sins,
He is faithful and just to forgive us our sins
and to cleanse us from all unrighteousness.

1 JOHN 1:9

FORGIVE AND RESTORE ME

Lord, show me any sin in my life so that I can confess it to You and be cleansed. Keep me undeceived in my heart and mind. Where I have sinned against You, I ask You to forgive and restore me.

〜 〜 〜

Confess your trespasses to one another,
and pray for one another, that you may be healed.

JAMES 5:16

I RENOUNCE UNFORGIVENESS

*L*ord, show me anyone against whom I have unforgiveness, and I will confess that unforgiveness to You as sin. Specifically, I pray about my relationship with (name anyone you need to forgive).

～ ～ ～

First be reconciled to your brother,
and then come and offer your gift.

MATTHEW 5:24

CREATE IN ME A CLEAN HEART

*L*ord, create in me a clean heart and renew a right spirit within me (Psalm 51:10). Set me free so that my heart can be clean when I come before You. I don't want anything to keep me from fulfilling Your ultimate purpose for my life.

෨ ෨ ෨

He who has clean hands and a pure heart...
shall receive blessing from the LORD,
and righteousness from the God of his salvation.

PSALM 24:4-5

Lord, help me to speak only words that are true, noble, just, pure, lovely, of good report, virtuous, excellent, or praiseworthy (Philippians 4:8). Help me to always be able to give the reason for the hope that is within me (1 Peter 3:15). Help me to speak the truth in love (Ephesians 4:15). Fill me with Your love so that it flows from me in the words I speak.

᭙ ᭙ ᭙

My tongue shall speak of Your righteousness
and of Your praise all the day long.

PSALM 35:28

BLESS MY FAMILY

*L*ord, I pray that You would bless my family and friends. Specifically, I lift up to You (name family members and friends). I also lift up to You my church family and the people I see in my work and throughout my day (name specific people who come to mind).

∽ ∽ ∽

Continue earnestly in prayer,
being vigilant in it with thanksgiving.

COLOSSIANS 4:2

YOU ARE MY PROVIDER

Lord, I ask that You would meet all my needs this day. Thank You that You have provided for my needs in the past and will continue to provide for me in the future, as You have promised in Your Word.

～ ～ ～

Ask, and it will be given to you; seek, and you will find;
knock, and it will be opened to you.
For everyone who asks receives,
and he who seeks finds, and to him who knocks
it will be opened.

MATTHEW 7:7-8

HELP ME TO LIVE IN YOUR WILL

*H*eavenly Father, help me to live in Your will. Thank You that Your will is not beyond knowing and that You reveal Yourself to me when I ask You to. Help me to abide in You so that I can understand Your ways and Your heart.

↩ ↩ ↩

By this we know that we abide in Him,
and He in us, because He has given us of His Spirit.

1 JOHN 4:13

PROVIDE OPPORTUNITIES FOR ME TO PRAY WITH OTHERS

*L*ord, You have said that when just two people are gathered in Your name, You are there in the midst of them (Matthew 18:20). What a wonderful promise to us. You have also said that when two of us *agree* in prayer, You will answer (Matthew 18:19). I pray You will help me to find someone with whom I can agree in prayer.

᪥ ᪥ ᪥

If two of you agree on earth
concerning anything that they ask,
it will be done for them by My Father in heaven.

MATTHEW 18:19

GIVE ME FAITH TO BELIEVE

*L*ord, I ask that You would send one or more persons into my life who are willing to pray with me on a regular basis. Let them be people who are trustworthy and mature in Your ways, and who have faith to believe that You answer prayer. Help me be sensitive as to whom they might be. Give me faith to believe for answers to all of our prayers.

∽ ∽ ∽

*If you have faith as a mustard seed,
you can say to this mulberry tree,
"Be pulled up by the roots and be planted
in the sea," and it would obey you.*

LUKE 17:6

GUIDE ME TO THE RIGHT PERSON

*L*ord, when I approach a person and ask them to pray with me, help me not to be hurt or offended if they refuse. Help me to be big enough to recognize that perhaps they were not the right person for that moment. Help me to pay attention to what *You* want instead of what *others* are thinking. Guide me to the right person with whom I can pray.

ᔐ ᔐ ᔐ

You will guide me with Your counsel.

PSALM 73:24

HELP ME TO HEAR YOU

Lord, work through me when I pray with another person so that I will pray right on target. Help me to hear Your Holy Spirit leading me and giving me knowledge, revelation, and discernment. Make me into a powerful prayer warrior.

∽ ∽ ∽

And this I pray, that your love may abound
still more and more in knowledge and all discernment.

PHILIPPIANS 1:9

*L*ord, give me boldness to ask for prayer from others. Help me to be honest in sharing my requests so that the issues are faced and problems are solved because we are able to pray in accordance with the truth.

᧥ ᧥ ᧥

Let us therefore come boldly to the throne of grace,
that we may obtain mercy
and find grace to help in time of need.

HEBREWS 4:16

HELP ME TO BE TRANSPARENT

*L*ord, I don't want to conceal things out of pride or fear that need to be revealed. I don't want to give a wrong picture about my situation in order to impress others. Help me to be fully transparent so that prayers for me can be fully powerful.

≈ ≈ ≈

Confess your trespasses to one another,
and pray for one another, that you may be healed.
The effective, fervent prayer
of a righteous man avails much.

JAMES 5:16

*L*ord, help me to recognize opportunities to pray with others that I might not otherwise have seen. Give me courage to pray for people so that I will not hesitate or hide from opportunities that present themselves. Help me to come alongside people in prayer the way You, Holy Spirit, come alongside me.

᷆ ᷆ ᷆

Bear one another's burdens,
and so fulfill the law of Christ.

GALATIANS 6:2

HELP ME UNDERSTAND THE POWER OF PRAYER

Lord, grow me up in knowledge of the power of prayer. As I reach out to pray with and for others, give me ever-increasing faith to believe for the answers. I know that with You, God, nothing is impossible.

෨ ෨ ෨

Whatever things you ask in prayer,
believing, you will receive.

MATTHEW 21:22

I WANT TO PRAY
ACCORDING TO YOUR WILL

*L*ord, give me confidence to bring my prayers before
You. Help me to trust Your willingness to hear and
respond. Enable me to pray according to Your will at all
times. My ultimate prayer is for Your will to be done in all
things.

∽ ∽ ∽

Now this is the confidence that we have in Him,
that if we ask anything according to His will,
He hears us. And if we know that He hears us,
whatever we ask, we know that we have
the petitions that we have asked of Him.

1 JOHN 5:14-15

HELP ME FIND STRONG BELIEVERS WITH WHOM I CAN PRAY

*L*ord, I ask that You would help me find a group of strong believers with whom I can pray regularly. Lead me to people who have their foundation built solidly on the Word of God and who have strong faith to believe for answers to their prayers. Show me if I am to lead such a group.

∽ ∽ ∽

I have given him as a witness to the people,
a leader and commander for the people.

ISAIAH 55:4

PREPARE ME TO LEAD OTHERS IN PRAYER

Lord, if You want me to lead a prayer or intercessory group, prepare me to do it well. Tell me where and when I should do it. May this prayer group be a positive and life-changing experience for everyone who is part of it.

↜ ↜ ↜

For God gives wisdom and knowledge and joy
to a man who is good in His sight.

ECCLESIASTES 2:26

KNIT OUR HEARTS TOGETHER IN UNITY

Lord, anytime I pray with others in a group, help us to come to a place of complete unity with one another. May we always be in one accord so that our prayers are powerful. Help us to submit to one another in the fear of God (Ephesians 5:21). Help us to "walk by the same rule" and "be of the same mind" (Philippians 3:16).

∽ ∽ ∽

Be of the same mind toward one another.

ROMANS 12:16

ENABLE US TO CONTINUE STEADFASTLY IN PRAYER

*H*eavenly Father, enable the members of any group I pray with to "be kindly affectionate to one another with brotherly love, in honor giving preference to one another; not lagging in diligence, fervent in spirit, serving the Lord; rejoicing in hope, patient in tribulation, continuing steadfastly in prayer" (Romans 12:10-12).

꙳ ꙳ ꙳

Let each of you look out not only for his own interests, but also for the interests of others.

PHILIPPIANS 2:4

MAY MY PRAYERS
BE PLEASING TO YOU

Lord, I want to always pray with Your clear leading and guidance. When I pray, give me great faith to believe for the answers. I know that without faith it is impossible to please You (Hebrews 11:6), and I want to please You more than anything else.

∽ ∽ ∽

Without faith it is impossible to please Him,
for he who comes to God must believe that He is,
and that He is a rewarder
of those who diligently seek Him.

HEBREWS 11:6

HELP ME TO ENCOURAGE OTHERS WITH MY PRAYERS

*L*ord, help me to be the kind of person who, by joining with others, is able to resist the onslaught of the enemy when he comes upon our lives like a torrential flash flood. May my faith be so strong that it gives rise to faith in others and encourages them to stand strong.

～ ～ ～

For we have great joy and consolation
in your love, because the hearts of the saints
have been refreshed by you.

PHILEMON 7

HELP ME TO TOUCH OTHERS WITH YOUR LOVE

Lord, help me to be a person who reaches out to touch others with Your love. Enable me to extend myself across cultural barriers, racial barriers, denominational barriers, and church barriers. I pray that I will never withdraw and separate myself from people who are not like me.

೬ ೬ ೬

He Himself is our peace, who has made both one,
and has broken down the middle wall of separation.

EPHESIANS 2:14

LEAD ME WHERE IT PLEASES YOU

*L*ord, help me to always be in the church You want me to be in, and enable me to become a part of the work You are doing there. I pray that I will always belong to a church that worships Your way, teaches Your Word in a clear and balanced manner, and understands the power of prayer.

∽ ∽ ∽

God has set the members, each one of them,
in the body just as He pleased.

1 CORINTHIANS 12:18

I PRAY FOR THE PASTORS
AND LEADERS OF MY CHURCH

*L*ord, guide the pastors and leaders of my church to be the men and women of God You created them to be. Help them to clearly understand the path You have for them. Help me and the rest of the congregation to catch their vision and do what is needed to support them. Protect them and provide for all their needs.

∽ ∽ ∽

I will give you shepherds according to My heart,
who will feed you with knowledge and understanding.

JEREMIAH 3:15

MAINTAIN UNITY IN OUR CHURCH

*L*ord, help me to move in unity with my church family
and enable us all to move together in harmony. Bring
redemption and restoration where it is needed. Thank
You that You are greater than any difficulty we might face,
and Your love guarantees that we will triumph over it.

∽ ∽ ∽

*Thanks be to God, who always leads us
in triumph in Christ, and through us diffuses
the fragrance of His knowledge in every place.*

2 CORINTHIANS 2:14

MAY WE BE A WORSHIPING PEOPLE

Lord, help me to be a praising person and teach us as a church to be a worshiping people. Instruct us in what we need to know about worship and prayer so that we can become the intercessors You have called us to be.

～ ～ ～

Oh come, let us worship and bow down;
let us kneel before the LORD our Maker.
For He is our God, and we are the people
of His pasture, and the sheep of His hand.

PSALM 95:6-7

I GIVE THANKS
FOR YOUR GOODNESS

*H*eavenly Father, I worship You because "You are worthy, O Lord, to receive glory and honor and power" (Revelation 4:11). I know it is good to give thanks to You in all things (Psalm 92:1) for this is Your will (1 Thessalonians 5:18). I lift up Your name this day, for You are great and good to all who seek You.

∾ ∾ ∾

Sing praise to the LORD, you saints of His,
and give thanks at the remembrance of His holy name.

PSALM 30:4

RAISE UP YOUR PRAYING CHURCH

*L*ord, I pray that You would pour out Your Spirit on my church. May each church in my town hear Your call to prayer and take their place to become part of Your powerful praying church worldwide. May they also reach out to one another in love so they can pray together in unity for the needs of our city.

∽ ∽ ∽

You are no longer strangers and foreigners,
but fellow citizens with the saints
and members of the household of God.

EPHESIANS 2:19

*L*ord, I invite You to reign in this city. Pour out Your Spirit upon everyone so that all people will be drawn to You. Make our streets safe from accidents and evil people. Bless and protect the children. Remind me to pray often, and show me how I can join in prayer with others to pray for this city as well.

∽ ∽ ∽

Far be it from me that I should sin against the LORD in ceasing to pray for you.

1 SAMUEL 12:23

YOU ARE OUR HELP IN TIMES OF TROUBLE

Lord, help us to not be afraid when bad things happen, knowing You are our refuge and our strength, a very present help in trouble. Even if the world falls apart, even though the mountains are carried into the midst of the sea, we don't have to fear. Raise us up to be Your powerful praying church.

∽ ∽ ∽

Give ear, O LORD, to my prayer; and attend to the voice of my supplications. In the day of my trouble I will call upon You, for You will answer me.

PSALM 86:6-7

*L*ord, I thank You for the privilege of speaking to You in prayer. Increase my faith to believe that I can make a difference in my country when I pray. Help me to comprehend the significance of standing in the gap not only for my family, church, and community where I work and live, but also for my city, state, and nation.

∽ ∽ ∽

Men always ought to pray and not lose heart.

LUKE 18:1

SHOW ME HOW TO PRAY

*L*ord, give me direction to know how to intercede in every situation and for every concern. Make me bold to ask. Enable me to pray according to Your will. Give me faith to believe that impossible things can happen when I pray. Forgive me when I have any doubt about Your ability to answer.

∾ ∾ ∾

Through Him we both have access
by one Spirit to the Father.

EPHESIANS 2:18

VISIT OUR CITY
WITH YOUR MERCY AND GRACE

Lord, I pray for a divine visitation of Your mercy and
grace upon my city_____, my
state_____, and my
nation_____. I declare You to be
Lord over these places. It is a privilege to be able to be a
part of affecting my city, state, and nation for Your glory.

෴ ෴ ෴

The inhabitants of one city shall go to another,
saying, "Let us continue to go and pray before the LORD."

ZECHARIAH 8:21

VISIT OUR NATION WITH PEACE

Lord, help me to understand my role as an intercessor for my country. Help me to be Your instrument of peace, healing, and deliverance. Give me strength to not give up or shrink back when I see enemy opposition. Grow me into being a powerful intercessor who understands the authority I have been given by You in prayer.

∽ ∽ ∽

Many peoples and strong nations
shall come to seek the LORD of hosts in Jerusalem,
and to pray before the LORD.

ZECHARIAH 8:22

I PLEAD FOR YOUR GRACE

*L*ord, pour out Your mercy upon our land instead of the judgment we all deserve. I am not pleading for Your grace because I think we have earned it. I come because my heart breaks for the brokenness of my nation's people. And I know You are a God who is merciful.

∽ ∽ ∽

I know that You are a gracious and merciful God,
slow to anger and abundant in lovingkindness,
One who relents from doing harm.

JONAH 4:2

RAISE UP AN ARMY OF PRAYER WARRIORS

Lord, raise up an army of prayer warriors who can be mobilized on a moment's notice so that we can move in unity and by the power of Your Spirit. Help us to understand the powerful weapon we have in Your Word as we move into battle in prayer. If *You* are for us, who can be against us (Romans 8:31)?

✄ ✄ ✄

For the weapons of our warfare are not carnal
but mighty in God for pulling down strongholds.

2 CORINTHIANS 10:4

POUR OUT YOUR SPIRIT ON OUR NATION

Lord, pour out Your Spirit upon this nation. Bring unbelievers to a saving knowledge of Your Son, Jesus. Prosper us and rain Your blessings upon us. Thank You that Your eyes are on the righteous, and Your ears are open to our prayers (1 Peter 3:12). May Your love and peace so rise in our hearts that it becomes our greatest testimony of Your goodness.

～ ～ ～

*Surely His salvation is near to those who fear Him,
that glory may dwell in our land.*

PSALM 85:9

MAY MY PRAYERS MAKE A DIFFERENCE

*L*ord, help me to have faith to believe that my prayers, along with the prayers of my brothers and sisters in Christ all over the world, will make a difference as we pray for other nations. Show me each day which country and which people You want me to pray for, and guide me in how to do that.

~ ~ ~

The LORD *is high above all nations, His glory above the heavens. Who is like the* LORD *our God, who dwells on high, who humbles Himself to behold the things that are in the heavens and in the earth?*

PSALM 113:4-6

RAISE UP GODLY LEADERS

Lord, I know from Your Word that it is You who raises up kings and removes them (Daniel 2:21). I pray that You would raise up godly and righteous leaders to rule each country. Thank You that the work of righteousness will be peace, and the effect of righteousness will be quietness and assurance forever (Isaiah 32:17).

$\sim$ $\sim$ $\sim$

Let every soul be subject to the governing authorities.
For there is no authority except from God,
and the authorities that exist are appointed by God.

ROMANS 13:1

HELP THE NATIONS TO EXIST IN PEACE

*L*ord, show us Your ways. Teach us Your paths. Lead us in Your truth and teach us, for You are the God of our salvation (Psalm 25:4-5). Enable the countries of the earth to come together and cooperate peacefully. Specifically, I pray for (name any countries where there is war or civil strife). Bring peace to these nations and people.

෬ ෬ ෬

God be merciful to us and bless us, and cause
His face to shine upon us, that Your way may
be known on earth, Your salvation among all nations.

PSALM 67:1-2

RAISE UP PEOPLE WHO WILL PREACH THE GOSPEL

*L*ord, raise up men and women in the body of Christ who will "go into all the world and preach the gospel to every creature" (Mark 16:15). Send messengers and missionaries to tell people who You are and what You have done for them. Pour Your Spirit upon them and anoint them to preach the gospel to the nations.

❧ ❧ ❧

Also I heard the voice of the Lord, saying:
"Whom shall I send, and who will go for Us?"
Then I said, "Here am I! Send me."

ISAIAH 6:8

YOU ARE THE LIGHT OF THE WORLD

*L*ord, You are the light of the world, and I declare You to be Lord over every nation of the earth. I know Your light will always prevail. Establish Your kingdom on earth and help us, Your children, to be a people through whom Your light shines and through whom You touch the world for Your glory.

෧ ෧ ෧

*You are the light of the world. A city that is set
on a hill cannot be hidden...Let your light so shine
before men, that they may see your good works
and glorify your Father in heaven.*

MATTHEW 5:14,16